Trusting God

With Your

Dream

SUZANNE ELIZABETH ANDERSON

Henry and George Press
Evergreen, Colorado

Suzanne Elizabeth Anderson

Trusting God with Your Dream:

ISBN-13: 978-1502460264

ISBN-10: 1502460262
Suzanne Elizabeth Anderson
Henry and George Press
PO Box 2465
Evergreen, Colorado 80437

Scripture quotations are taken from the (NIV) New International Version, Copyright 1984, the International Bible Society. Used by permission. All rights reserved worldwide.
Also from The Message, by Eugene H. Peterson, 2005.

Cover Design © www.canva.com
Cover illustration: Gabor from Hungary via morguefile.com

Published by Henry and George Press
www.henryandgeorgepress.com

For more devotional readings and to find out about upcoming books:
www.suzanneelizabethanderson.com

For Julie Carlson

My dear friend and a sister in Christ,
With gratitude for your friendship and the years
we've spent talking and laughing,
sharing answered and unanswered prayers.

Suzanne Elizabeth Anderson

Table of Contents

Introduction

One Christmas, my mother gave me a copy of *The Daily Walk Bible.* I'd tried daily reading-plan Bibles before but without the dedication to make it beyond January. But this time, with *The Daily Walk Bible,* was different.

What kept me motivated, as I slogged through those difficult Old Testament books, was that I'd reached a crossroads in my life, and I was seeking life-changing responses to my unanswered prayers about where my life was going.

God had gone silent when I needed Him most, and I was trying to find out why. Although I believed I'd prayed in good faith and prayed "without ceasing", it seemed that nothing I did brought an answer to my prayers. It wasn't that God wasn't there; He just wasn't listening to me.

After a year in the Bible, I came to a startling realization. All this time that I was waiting on God for an answer, I wasn't waiting alone. God was with me.

God used my year of waiting not to frustrate me, or abandon me, but to draw me into a closer relationship with Him.

As you read through these 31 days of devotionals, I pray that you too will be drawn closer to God.

In these pages, you will discover:

God will always provide an answer to your prayer.

You are never alone; God is always near.

And more than anything else . . .

God loves you beyond measure.

$\mathcal{D}ay$ 1

But I am trusting you, O Lord,

Saying, "**You are my God!**"

My future is in Your hands.

~Psalm 31:14-15

Day 1

TRUSTING GOD WITH YOUR DREAM

Talk about a dive into the deep end. What a great way to start our devotional journey!

Do we trust God enough not only to say the words in this Bible verse, but also to believe them and live them?

"You are my God, my future is in Your hands!"

If you're not quite ready to make this commitment to God today, let's make it our goal to be there at the end of 31 days together.

If you're like me and have tried to do everything on your own, the most difficult decision may be letting go of your future and letting God shape it to His will.

What an enormous amount of trust it takes to say, "Okay God, I've tried to do it my way, but I'm ready to let go of the reins and turn my life over to You."

My first reaction to that announcement has always been: *But what if I don't like the plans God has for my life?*

Don't worry. We're going to tackle that question, too.

This conflict, of asking for God's help but not totally trusting His ability or willingness to answer, was what finally made me turn to the Bible in search of guidance and to many, many hours of prayer to seek God. In the end, I was able to say, "God, You're in charge of my school life, my social life, my whole life".

In the past, I tried to do it all myself. With mixed results.

Today, I declare that I am asking for God's blessing on my future and that I trust in Him to work it out for the best.

Will you join me to trust God with your present and your future? What are you willing to turn over to God during our 31-day journey together?

Day 2

"You intended to harm me,
but God intended it for good
to accomplish what is now being
done..."

~Genesis 50:20

Day 2

GOD INTENDED IT FOR GOOD

So where should we start on this journey toward a closer relationship with God?

How about right where we are?

It's that space in between when we first release our prayers to God and the moment when God answers.

At times, it can feel like the loneliest place on Earth because it's just us, alone with our unanswered prayers.

So let's start there. Alone and wondering, "Why is this happening, God?"

Whether I'm the one who got myself into the mess or not, my first instinct often involves asking God for help.

But what about those times when, despite our best efforts, we find ourselves in a dilemma that we've prayed about but received no answer?

Where is God then?

What can we do when things look bleak, and we feel most alone?

God promises that no matter how dismal the picture, He will take our problem and turn it into an opportunity for our growth.

And an opportunity to grow closer to God.

No matter where you are in your personal relationship with God, I believe that if you spend the next month walking with God through His holy word and meeting Him in the quiet of prayer, you will come out stronger, hope-filled, and with a new answer to your prayers.

Let's start with this outrageous promise from God: Whatever you are going through today, God will work it out for your good.

Day 3

8 All of those Levites read parts of the Scroll of the Law of God to the people. They made it clear to them. They told them what it meant. So the people were able to understand what was being read.

9 Then Nehemiah and Ezra spoke up. So did the Levites who were teaching the people. All of those men said to the people, "This day is set apart to honor the Lord your God. So don't sob. Don't be sad." All of the people had been sobbing as they listened to the words of the Law. Nehemiah was governor. Ezra was a priest and a teacher of the law.

10 Nehemiah said, **"Go and enjoy some good food and sweet drinks. Send some of it to those who don't have any. This day is set apart to honor our Lord. So don't be sad. The joy of the Lord makes you strong." Nem 8:8-10**

Day 3

GOD'S JOY

When waiting for an answer to prayer, it's easy to get discouraged. Sometimes it feels like we're walking around with a dark cloud overhead. When we're waiting, we can't see an end to our worry or our wondering if things will work out.

During this time of waiting, the worst thing that can happen is that our anxiety can balloon until it becomes all-consuming, and we are so consumed with trying to figure out a solution, that we are unable to find joy in any area of our life.

The first time I heard this short, sweet verse from Nehemiah, it took my breath away. I was sitting in church, feeling discouraged about a prayer that I was waiting to be answered, and I was so involved in my own thoughts that I really wasn't paying close attention to what was being said. And then, thank God, this verse broke through my jumbled thoughts and brought everything into perspective.

When we are in a period of waiting, we might not be able to change our circumstances or hurry the outcome, but that doesn't mean that it should steal our joy. Because, as this verse assures us:

The joy of the Lord makes us strong.

We don't have to rely on our own strength; God's strength is more than enough to sustain us. Lean on Him. Seek God in prayer and ask Him to share His joy and His strength with you.

God's joy can fill our days with gladness until we receive the answer we are waiting for.

$\mathcal{D}$ay 4

The Lord said to Moses,

"Tell Aaron and his sons,

'This is how you are to bless the Israelites.

Say to them:

"The Lord bless you and keep you;

the Lord make his face shine upon you

and be gracious to you;

the Lord turn his face toward you and give you peace." '

"So they will put My name on the Israelites,

and I will bless them."

~Num 6:22-27

$\mathcal{D}$ay 4

GOD WANTS TO BLESS YOU

What is the first thought that comes to mind when you wake every day?

Are you thankful for another day, or do you wake to worries about how you are going to handle the pressures of school, or your job, or the important relationships in your life? Are you following God or following peer pressure down a dangerous path?

We are blessed when we can turn to friends and family to seek their support or another perspective during trying times.

We can also gain comfort in knowing that God waits with open arms to offer us His blessing.

God blesses us with peace, with love that is never-ending, and with the strength to face any challenge.

Knowing that God is the Provider of Limitless Blessing, I'd like to challenge you, in the midst of your own trials, to ask how you can bless someone else today.

Is there someone in your life who could use a phone call just to say, "I'm thinking of you"? Or an elderly neighbor who would welcome a gift of a homemade meal delivered to his or her door today?

Is there a thrift store in your community that would love to have a donation of your gently worn clothing to support charities in your community?

I'm giving you this challenge because I've found that when I help someone else, I am blessed with a feeling joy and gratitude. Try it and see how God will bless you, too.

Day 5

The Lord said to Moses, "Take the staff, and you and your brother Aaron gather the assembly together. Speak to that rock before their eyes and it will pour out its water. You will bring water out of the rock for the community so they and their livestock can drink."

So Moses took the staff from the Lord's presence, just as He commanded him. He and Aaron gathered the assembly together in front of the rock and Moses said to them, "Listen, you rebels, must we bring you water out of this rock?" Then Moses raised his arm and struck the rock twice with his staff. Water gushed out, and the community and their livestock drank.

But the Lord said to Moses and Aaron, "Because you did not trust in Me enough to honor Me as holy in the sight of the Israelites, you will not bring this community into the land I have given them."

~Num 20:8-12

$\mathcal{D}$ay 5

TRUST IN
GOD'S DIRECTION

When I first read the summary at the start of today's reading, I thought, 'why is God being so harsh? Who cares whether Moses spoke to the rock or struck it? Why should he be denied seeing the Promised Land?'

Then I spoke with my mother, and she pointed out that God was not only asking Moses for obedience but also for trust. And He asks the same of us.

In fact, as God plainly says, "Because you did not trust in Me enough to honor Me . . ." And that's the bottom line.

Trust is essential to obedience. You can't have one without the other.

It is impossible to have faith in God, if you don't also trust in God's words and the promises that He makes throughout the Bible. And that's the greatest challenge we have right now; we need to learn to trust in God.

It's easy to read the Bible and agree with the lessons, especially when they don't pertain to us.

But when we take up the challenge of applying God's Word to our lives, it can stop us in our tracks. Suddenly, we wonder if what we are reading is really what God wants to tell us. This can challenge our faith, especially when we read isn't what we wanted to hear. How can we be sure?

As we read in today's verses, **God may withhold an answer to prayer until we relinquish control of the outcome and put our complete trust in Him.**

Are you willing to trust God with the outcome of your prayers? Are you willing to trust God with your dream?

If not, what's holding you back?

Today, talk to God and share your doubts and fears.

Then, be still and listen closely to what God says to you.

Day 6

The Lord said to Moses,

"How long will these people treat Me with contempt?

How long will they refuse to believe in Me, in spite of all the miraculous signs I have performed among them?

I will strike them down with a plague and destroy them, but I will make you into a nation greater and stronger than they."

~Num 14:11

Jesus replied, "Truly I tell you, if you have faith and do not **doubt**, not only can you do what was done to the fig tree, but also you can say to this mountain, 'Go, throw yourself into the sea,' and it will be done.

~Matthew 21:21

$\mathcal{D}ay$ 6

RELEASE DOUBT

During a difficult time, how often do we lose our faith in God? How often do we doubt Him?

Perhaps the most difficult problem in our walk with God is to trust that He has our best interests in mind when all we can see are great obstacles.

God led the Israelites to the Promised Land. He gave them the dream they'd hoped for and worked toward.

However, they didn't believe that God would keep His promise and deliver them safely into the land, so they refused to accept the gift they'd been given. Their lack of faith cost them another forty years of misery.

Can we learn to trust God, even when things look impossible?

When circumstances look their worst, instead of reacting to God's silence by turning our back on Him, can we draw closer to Him?

Can we seek Him out, again and again?

In the verse from Matthew, Jesus answers our questions with a resounding "Yes!" If only we are able to have faith. Faith in God to answer our prayers. Faith in our ability to keep moving forward until we receive that answer. Faith that not does God know our dream, He is the author of our dream.

I believe our faith can move mountains.

But because that kind of faith is so powerful, it can also be very scary to believe in, to embrace, and to give wholly to God. Especially when that faith surrounds our most desperately offered prayers.

Still, during these moments, I believe that when we turn toward God, He will respond. We will be comforted by His nearness.

Day 7

The Lord your God has blessed you in all the work of your hands.

He has watched over your journey through this vast desert.

These forty years the Lord you God has been with you,

and you have not lacked anything.

~Deuteronomy 2:7

Day 7

REMEMBER GOD'S PAST PROVISION

When we are in the middle of our own spiritual desert, it may help us to remember the times when God has been with us and taken care of us, so that we can believe that He will take care of us even now.

Take a moment right now to recall times when God has supplied your needs, both great and small. How about the phone call from a friend who calls to say 'hello' on a day when you feel so alone? Or the acceptance letter to a college after you received five rejection letters from other schools and wondered if you'd be able to attend college next year?

God is always with us. From the big events, like the negative medical test result, to the little ones, like the bus that shows up to get us to work on time when we're running late.

When we are in the midst of our current crisis, it's easy to feel overwhelmed because it feels like life has always gone wrong for us. That we've always failed or been without. And it seems impossible to imagine that it will ever get better.

Create a list of ten moments when God has provided for your needs just in time or when they were most needed. Or when He has answered a prayer that you thought would never be answered.

By recalling God's past provision, we can reassure ourselves that what **He has done in the past, He will do again in the future.**

Day 8

Though the Lord gave you adversity
for food and suffering for drink,
He will still be with you to teach you.
You will see your teacher with your
own eyes.
Your own ears will hear Him.
Right behind you a voice will say,
"This is the way you should go,"
whether to the right or to the left.
~Isaiah 30:20-22

The Lord is my shepherd, I lack nothing. He makes me lie down in green pastures, He leads me beside quiet waters, He refreshes my soul. He guides me along the right paths for His name's sake.

Even though I walk through the darkest valley,

I will fear no evil, for You are with me; Your rod and Your staff, they comfort me.

You prepare a table before me in the presence of my enemies. You anoint my head with oil; my cup overflows.

Surely Your goodness and love will follow me all the days of my life, and I will dwell in the house of the Lord forever.

~Psalm 23

Day 8

GOD IS WITH US

If we are in the middle of a valley of doubt and despair and can't see our way forward, it's natural to wonder where God is when we need Him most.

When we have shared our deepest secret, our dream, our heart's desire with God, we suddenly feel vulnerable. Will God answer us?

When all we feel is alone, it's difficult to believe that God is really with us.

As you read through the rest of these daily devotionals, let the Bible scriptures speak to your heart.

Write down your favorites on a note card and place them on your desk or on your dresser or next to the window in the kitchen, anywhere you will be able to see them several times a day.

As we wait with God for an answer to our prayers, we are also working with God, moving forward to a solution. During these times when we can't readily measure our progress, having God's scripture always in front of our eyes will be a constant reminder that we are not alone. That God will guide us through as long as we call on Him to direct our steps.

I truly believe that when we face our darkest moments, **if we will turn to God in prayer and seek His comfort through His Word, we will find our hearts and minds healed.**

$\mathcal{D}$ay 9

Then the Lord said to Moses,
"I will rain down bread from heaven
for you.
The people are to go out each day and
gather enough for that day.
In this way I will test them
and see whether they will follow My
instructions."

~Exodus 16:4

$\mathcal{D}$ay 9

ENOUGH FOR TODAY

When we are praying for an answer, we of course want the whole problem solved. We want a job restored, a sickness healed, a love returned.

We want God to make it all better in an instant, and sometimes, that is what we receive. But most times, especially when God is working something out in our lives, we receive just enough for the day.

On those occasions, just enough can feel so small that we don't recognize it as God's providence or part of His greater plan for our lives.

At those times, it's very easy to become impatient or even resentful and wonder why God isn't providing a complete solution.

When the Israelites were wandering through the desert and had run out of food, they cried out to Moses, who turned to God. And God provided for their needs, a lesson that is echoed later in the teachings of Jesus Christ, who says, "I will provide for all your needs."

When we are in the desert and see no source to provide for ourselves, will we trust God to provide the solution?

And are we willing to obey God's instructions?

Can we be patient and grateful when God provides enough for the day?

$\mathcal{D}ay$ 10

Do not let this Book of the Law depart from your mouth;

meditate on it day and night,

so that you may be careful to do everything written in it.

Then you will be prosperous and successful.

Have I not commanded you?

Be strong and courageous.

Do not be terrified; do not be discouraged,

for the Lord your God will be with you wherever you go."

~Joshua 1:8-9

Day 10

HE SAVES US

As I mentioned in the Introduction, the greatest gift I received during my walk through the Bible was discovering that God is always with us.

He never forsakes us.

He never leaves us.

I believe that God longs to take care of us, to show us every day that we are dearly loved.

The greatest gifts that God longs to give us are the love, salvation, and eternal life provided through the death and resurrection of His Son, Jesus.

Best of all, receiving this gift is incredibly easy. When we receive the love of God that was manifested through the sacrifice of His Son, Jesus, we receive the forgiveness of our sins and a perfect salvation that means we will never be separated from God's love.

Have you asked God to forgive you of your sins, to come into your heart, and to heal your broken places?

If not, let's pray together now: Jesus, I thank You for dying for my sins and for rising again to give me new life through You. I ask You to forgive me of my sins, **I accept Your salvation, and I want You to come into my heart and be my Lord forever. Amen.**

Day 11

Submit to God and be at peace with
Him;
in this way prosperity will come to
you.
Accept instruction from His mouth
and lay up His words in your heart.

If you return to the Almighty you will
be restored;
If you remove wickedness far from
your tent and assign your nuggets to
the dust,
your gold of Ophir to the rocks in the
ravines, then the Almighty will be
your gold, the choicest silver for you.

Surely then you will find delight in
the Almighty and will lift up your face
to God.

You will pray to Him, and He will
hear you, and you will fulfill your
vows.
What you decide on will be done,
and light will shine on your ways.
~Job 22:21-29

Day 11

PRAYING GOD'S WORDS BACK TO HIM

Submit to God and be at peace with Him;
in this way prosperity will come to you.

Today's verses speak to me because this firm faith is something I am struggling with at the moment. Like Job, I am searching for evidence that these things are true. I am sowing the seeds but not yet seeing the fruits of my labor.

When we are in the middle of an unanswered prayer, it's difficult to 'be at peace' with God.

Then, in the very next verse, we are encouraged to store the Word of God in our hearts and accept His instruction. I believe that's exactly what we need to do when we are in the depths of unknowing.

It's during these times, when we are called on to trust God the most, that we have the greatest opportunity to grow in our relationship with Him and to grow as individuals.

Open your Bible, find a verse that speaks to your situation, and pray that verse right back to God as if it was written from your perspective.

You will pray to Him, and He will hear you,
and you will fulfill your vows.
What you decide on will be done,
and light will shine on your ways.

. . . becomes:

I will pray to God, and He will hear me,

and I will fulfill my vows.
What I've decided will be done,
and light will shine on my ways.

I believe that when we pray God's Word back to Him, with a humble spirit, we will be drawn into a closer communion with Him and will find not only answers to our prayers but also the peace that comes from God's love.

Day 12

May He give you the desire of your
heart

and make all your plans succeed.

We will shout for joy when you are
victorious

and will lift up our banners in the
name of our God.

May the Lord grant all your requests.

~Psalm 20:4-5

$\mathcal{D}$ay 12

THE DESIRES OF
YOUR HEART

Yes, someday our prayers will be answered, and we will be victorious.

When this verse says we will "lift our banners up in the name of our God," I believe that is the true key to making our dreams succeed.

If we can launch our plans 'in the name of God', meaning that we are dedicating their outcome to God and trusting Him for the results, we can also trust God for the rest of the verse, i.e. the desires of our hearts.

In other words, **when the desires of our heart are aligned with God's plans for our lives, we can trust Him completely for the outcome.**

Have you dedicated your dream in the name of God? If you haven't, try it today and be willing to listen to what you hear in response. Often when we ask God for His blessing, we will receive a 'gut feeling' about whether or not what we're asking for is really something God would want us involved in.

When you come to God in prayer and lay out the desires of your heart, do you take time to listen in silence to see if your plans are also God's will for your life?

Ask God to "direct your steps" today, to bring your plans alongside His plans for you.

Day 13

When my heart was grieved

and my spirit embittered,

I was senseless and ignorant;

I was a brute beast before you.

Yet I am always with You;

You hold me by my right hand.

You guide me with Your counsel,

and afterward You will take me

into glory.

~ Psalm 73:21-24

Day 13

I AM ALWAYS
WITH YOU

Ever had one of those days when you woke up and felt depressed, when everything seemed overwhelming?

I have. More often than I'd like to admit.

The first verse today perfectly reflected what the depths of those hopeless days feel like to me.

I'm sharing this because I want you to understand that trusting God with our dream means having the courage to share all of our thoughts and feelings with Him.

All of them. Yes, even the ugly, embarrassing, *you'd-be-mortified-if-your-mother-or-best-friend-knew-you-had-such thoughts and feelings.*

Don't be afraid that God can't handle your anger or fear or tears. He can and He will.

Really. God is already aware of all of your thoughts.

So **why am I suggesting you sit down and pour out your heart to God?** Why do I think confessing all of these horrible, tearful, angry thoughts to God will actually do wonders for your relationship with God?

When you honestly share all of your emotions with God, you will find that your anger and sadness will become lighter and will be replaced with a spirit of God's love for you. When you dump all of those thoughts, you'll be making room in your heart and mind for more of God's thoughts about you, for His love for you.

When there is less of your negative noise buzzing in the background, there is more space for God's voice to reach you.

As I poured out my heart, God showed His presence time and time again. By the end of the day, I truly felt at peace.

Which is exactly the promise that we read in the second paragraph. No matter how petulant we become, God is always with us; He will guide us through the tough times if we just take His hand and walk with Him.

Thank You, God.

Day 14

I love God because He listened to
me,

listened as I begged for mercy.

He listened so intently

as I laid out my case before Him.

~ Psalm 116

Day 14

GOD IS LISTENING

Today's verse reminds me of a walk through the woods yesterday. As my dogs and I walked through a grove of Aspen, I talked out loud to God about my career plans, my need for an affirmation that I am on the right path, and that I will be able to make a go of this.

Unfortunately, I didn't hear an answer. In fact, I'm not sure I can say I've ever heard a word from God.

I know some people who have, and I believe my problem is that I'm not very good at listening.

I'm very good at talking.

One of my greatest struggles in my relationship with God is feeling like I never hear from Him. I'm never quite sure that He's directing my steps, because I never hear His directions.

Which is exactly why I believe that after we've poured out our hearts to God, we need to sit quietly and listen.

Today's verse was a reassurance that even though I can't hear Him speaking to me, God is still listening. And because His mercy and patience are infinite, He will continue to listen as long as we need to talk.

God will continue to listen for as long as it takes us to finally get to a place where we are ready to listen to Him.

The next time you're feeling as if your prayers aren't being heard, try a long silent walk through the woods, or try sitting in silence. (Can't find a quiet corner at home? Your local library might be a good place to spend a quiet hour.) As you walk, or sit, in silence, turn your thoughts inward, invite the Holy Spirit to come into your heart and speak to you, and then listen for the gentle whisper of God.

Day 15

Yet Jerusalem says, "The Lord has deserted us; the Lord has forgotten us."

Never! Can a mother forget her nursing child?
Can she feel no love for the child she has borne?
But even if that were possible,
I would not forget you!
See, I have written your name on the palms of My hands.
~ Isaiah 48:12-16

"Therefore I tell you, do not worry about your life, what you will eat or drink; or about your body, what you will wear.

Is not life more than food, and the body more than clothes?

Look at the birds of the air; they do not sow or reap or store away in barns, and yet your heavenly Father feeds them.

Are you not much more valuable than they?"

~Matthew 6:25-26

Day 15

DON'T WORRY,
BE THANKFUL

When everything feels overwhelming, it can be difficult to believe that anything is going right! This passage is a reminder that God is ever present and cares for us.

Which is why we need perspective. Pronto.

This is why keeping a Gratitude Journal can be so effective.

If you are willing to spend ten minutes recalling things that are going right, that you are actually happy about, you can turn your attitude around.

By remembering how much we have to be grateful for, we remind ourselves how beautifully God is already providing for our current needs.

"Can any one of you by worrying add a single hour to your life?"
~Matthew 6:27

As this verse suggests, we can let go of worry because worry isn't going to change our circumstances. We can rest in the assurance that God provides for all our needs, and we can replace worthless worrying with more productive thoughts.

This shift in thinking will improve our attitudes, which in turn can help us make better decisions, take action, and move more quickly toward our goals.

Write down five things about your current circumstances for which you are grateful. Afterward, take a moment to thank God not only for His provision but also for helping you to appreciate what He has provided.

We've reached the halfway point in our journey. Will you commit to finish out the remaining days, continuing your daily gratitude list?

I believe this exercise will change your approach to each day and bring greater blessings into your life.

$\mathcal{D}$ay 16

Always be full of joy in the Lord. I say it again—rejoice! Let everyone see that you are considerate in all you do. Remember, the Lord is coming soon.

Don't worry about anything; instead, pray about everything.

Tell God what you need, and **thank** Him for all He has done.

Then you will experience God's peace, which exceeds anything we can understand.

His peace will guard your hearts and minds as you live in Christ Jesus.

And now, dear brothers and sisters, one final thing. Fix your thoughts on what is true, and honorable, and right, and pure, and lovely, and admirable.

Think about things that are excellent and worthy of praise. *~Philippians 4:4-10*

$\mathcal{D}$ay 16

FIX YOUR THOUGHTS

I believe these verses contain a simple, yet profoundly effective, recipe for success in life. Don't believe me?

Well, let's pull them apart and see what God is recommending for a more fruitful life:

1. "Don't worry about anything; instead, pray about everything."

2. Communicate with God: "Tell Him what you need."

3. Recall your gratitude: "Thank Him for all He's done."

4. Stay focused on your goal: "Fix your thoughts."

5. Praise God and remain positive: "Always be full of joy in the Lord. I say it again—rejoice!"

6. Share God's goodness with others: "Let everyone see that you are considerate in all you do."

7. The result: "You will experience God's peace, which exceeds anything we can understand. His peace will guard your hearts and minds as you live in Christ Jesus."

Stop for a moment, close your eyes, and imagine what your life would look like if you truly lived these principles each day?

Would you worry less? Would others enjoy being with you more? Would you be able to draw closer to God? Do you think you would feel happier?

$\mathcal{D}$ay 17

Has God forgotten to be gracious?

Has He slammed the door on His compassion?

And I said, "This is my fate;

the Most High has turned His

hand against me."

But then I recall all You have done

O Lord; I remember Your wonderful

deeds of long ago.

They are constantly in my thoughts.

I cannot stop thinking about Your

mighty works.

~ Psalm 77:9-12

And now, just as you accepted Christ Jesus as your Lord, you must continue to follow Him. Let your roots grow down into Him, and let your lives be built on Him. Then your faith will grow strong in the truth you were taught, and you will overflow with thankfulness.

~ *Colossians 2:6-7*

$\mathcal{D}$ay 17

GROW INTO GOD

Two days ago, we discussed keeping a Gratitude Journal to bring to mind our many blessings, even in the midst of our turmoil.

Today I want to expand on that idea and suggest that you write a letter.

Begin with "Dear God:"

And then, writing as fast as you can, so that your mind can't censor your words, pour out your thoughts, the good, the bad, and the ugly. Share everything with God.

That's what we've found in the first of today's passages. The writer is pouring out his heart to his Lord: *Where has God gone? Has He turned His back on me? Has God forgotten me? Left me without hope?*

That raw honesty is what God wants from us if we are to have a truly honest relationship with Him.

I suggest you write this part of your letter to God as fast as you can because sometimes it's embarrassing for us to really express our heartfelt emotions to God. We are taught to view God as a stern father-figure, instead of a loving, compassionate God who loves us without ending.

Once you've emptied yourself of your pain, end this letter with your list of gratitude and praise to God, just as the Psalmist recalls God's "wonderful deeds of long ago".

And finally, the verse in Colossians reminds us that after we have received Christ as our savior, we must grow in our relationship with Him. We must "let our roots grow" so that we can create a foundation that will see us through troubling times.

That is my hope for you. As you pour out your heart to God and thank Him for the blessings you have already received, you will grow closer to God and receive a relationship that will last a lifetime and beyond.

When we pursue God, He rewards us with love and a relationship that will grow deeper over time. He promises invites us into a relationship that will never fade and will enrich our lives until our very last day on Earth.

$\mathcal{D}ay18$

Stop at the crossroads and look around.

Ask for the old, Godly way, and walk in it.

Travel its path, and you will find rest for your souls. But you reply, 'No, that's not the road we want!'

I posted watchmen over you who said, 'Listen for the sound of the alarm.'

But you replied, 'No! We won't pay attention!'

~ *Jeremiah 6:16-17*

Don't let anyone capture you with empty philosophies and

high-sounding nonsense that come from

human thinking and from the spiritual

power of this world, rather than from Christ.

For in Christ lives all the fullness

of God in a human body. So you also are

complete though your union with Christ, who is the

head over every ruler and authority.

~ Colossians 2:8-10

$\mathcal{D}$ay 18

WALKING A GODLY PATH

Lately, I've switched back and forth from one Bible translation to another. This helps me to read old familiar verses from a fresh perspective.

During my year of reading through the Bible, I often found that a reading in the New Testament echoed a message that spoke to me first in that day's Old Testament reading.

That was the case with today's reading.

What practical advice I received in the passage from Jeremiah!

It reminded me that so often I ask God for an answer to prayer, and then when I receive it, I say, "No, no, that's not what I had in mind. I wanted a different answer."

As if answers from God were like slips of paper pulled from a fortune cookie. If you don't like the first answer, open the next cookie and see what that one says.

In this passage, God reminds us that if we walk in the Godly path He has shown us, everything will work out.

The New Testament passage from Colossians expands on this lesson by reminding us that we shouldn't get caught up in the latest fads in thought, in trying to find our own way, but that through Christ, we have all that we need and that He will guide us.

$\mathcal{D}$ay 19

I'll show up and take care of you as I promised and bring you back home. I know what I'm doing. I have it all planned out; plans to take care of you, not abandon you, plans to give you the future you hope for.

When you call on Me, when you come and pray to Me, I'll listen.
When you come looking for Me, you'll find Me.
Yes, when you get serious about finding Me and want it more than anything else, I'll make sure you won't be disappointed. *~Jeremiah 29:11-13*

Day 19

GOD WILL
SHOW UP

This verse is probably familiar to you. I've read it in several translations, and it never ceases to inspire me with hope when I feel stuck and in need of reassurance.

When we are learning to trust God with our dream, it can feel as if nothing is happening. Perhaps everything starts out great, we shoot out of the block and think that nothing can stop us.

Until it does.

Suddenly we come to a complete stop. It feels like no matter what we try, we're not making progress on our dream.

What is worse than that? It can feel like our prayers are not being heard.

We pray, "**How much longer do I have to wait, God**?"

And receive only silence in return.

When we can't see the way forward, it's reassuring to have a reminder that God has a plan, that is perfect for each one of us. He will carry out our personalized-perfect-plan if we are obedient to His Will and allow Him to work in our lives.

That trust, that willingness to continue working in faith, even when we don't know how it's all going to turn out, is our challenge today.

Keep working.

Keep your eyes on God's Will for your life.

God will show up.

$\mathcal{D}$ay 20

All Scripture is inspired by God and is

useful to teach us

what is true and to make

us realize what is wrong in our lives.

It corrects us when we are wrong and

teaches us to do what is right.

God uses it to prepare and equip

his people to do every good work.

~ 2 Timothy 3:16-17

I cried out, "I am slipping!"

but Your unfailing love, O Lord,

supported me.

When doubts filled my mind,

Your comfort gave me renewed

hope and cheer. *~ Psalm 94:18-19*

$\mathcal{D}$ay 20

THANK GOD FOR UNANSWERED PRAYERS

My favorite verses in the Bible are the ones that remind me of God's love and of His desire to answer our prayers and provide the "desires of our hearts".

But today's verse, from 2nd Timothy, is a reminder that God's Word is also there to show us what is wrong in our lives. As result, some of our prayers will not be answered with a "yes" from God when they violate His laws or when they are not in His perfect plan for our life.

When we face this conflict between what we want and what God's Word teaches, it can create some of the most difficult moments in our walk with God.

We feel like crying out, "Why, God?" because we can't see the bigger picture. We can only feel our heart breaking, it feels like our world is crumbling, and our disappointment in that moment may feel so overwhelming we wonder how we will survive.

But we will. If we turn all of that pain over to God and ask Him to show us His better plan for our lives. The one that is so wonderful, we can't even imagine it. But God can. He already has.

As I look back on my life, I understand now that there were some very **important moments when my unanswered prayer was actually God's greatest blessing.** He was subtly steering me in the way He wanted me to go because His plan was so much better than what I was asking for with my shortsighted vision.

How about you? Can you recall a few prayers that you are now happy God said "No" to?

As we go through the day, let's recall this verse:

When doubts filled my mind,
Your comfort gave me renewed
hope and cheer.

What an encouraging message to know that God is with us throughout the day to lift us up and remind us that He is our greatest cheerleader, that He believes in us even when we lose confidence in our own abilities.

When we face a "no" from God or an unanswered prayer, and doubt fills our mind, let's remember those same answers held unexpected blessings from God in the past. Remember, God only wants the very best for us!

Day 21

The Lord is compassionate and
merciful,
slow to get angry and filled with
unfailing love.
He will not constantly accuse us,
nor remain angry forever.
He does not punish us for all
our sins;
He does not deal harshly with us,
as we deserve.

For His unfailing love toward those
who fear Him
is as great as the height of the
heavens above the earth.
He has removed our sins as far
from us
as the east is from the west.

The Lord is like a father to
His children,
tender and compassionate to
those who fear Him.
~ *Psalm 103:8-12*

Day 21

LET GO
OF SHAME

How often do we hold onto guilt or shame for our sins long after everyone else has moved on? Instead of learning from our mistakes, asking for forgiveness, and moving forward, why do we wallow in our despair?

I know that this is a terrific challenge for me.

Sometimes I wonder if I get some enjoyment from wallowing in my past mistakes, since I spend so much time doing it instead of fixing the problem and forgetting it.

It's important for us to learn from past mistakes so that we don't repeat them in the future.

Yet once we've learned, we need to move forward. Wallowing in the past will keep us stuck in the past and incapable of moving into the fresh start God has planned for us in the present.

Today's verses remind me that **God, in His infinite wisdom, forgives our sins in the blink of an eye** because He can see the big picture. He knows that we have an entire lifetime to make mistakes and do better. Sometimes we will fail, but if we accept responsibility, ask forgiveness, and go forward to do better, we will mature as individuals.

Let us accept God's forgiveness, seek the forgiveness of those we've hurt, and forgive ourselves at the same time. After all, if you forgave a friend for some transgression, wouldn't you feel offended if the next time you saw them, they were still dwelling on the same issue?

God sees us as He created us, with all our faults but also with all our strengths and beauty. After all, we are His children.

$\mathcal{D}$ay 22

A stone is heavy and sand is weighty, but the **resentment** caused by a fool is even heavier.

~ Proverbs 27:3

$\mathcal{D}$ay 22

HOW TO DEAL WITH JEALOUSY AND RESENTMENT

As I made my way through today's Bible readings, nothing jumped out and inspired me. Until I reached this final little verse from Proverbs.

Wow!

This verse hit me right between the eyes and convicted me about the way I've been feeling over the past few days.

I've been restless, looking backward instead of forward, feeling regret, impatient, and yes, resentful. And if I'm being very honest, jealous of people who seem to have achieved so easily, the dream I want so badly.

When I'm working on a big project, like the novel I'm currently writing, I need hours of uninterrupted quiet time at my computer to concentrate on the story. When that time gets interrupted and things don't go exactly as I'd planned, I get discouraged and impatient.

When I see someone who makes success look easy, while I struggle with failure, jealousy can blind me to seeing anything other than my own shortcomings.

Jealousy and resentment are like weights that sit on your chest, a constant reminder that you are not happy. Instead of keeping our focus on our dream, or better yet, on God's Will for our lives, we are consumed with watching someone else.

When my thoughts are consumed with thoughts of jealousy or resentment, not only do I lose time away from pursuing my dream, I resent the person or thing that pulled me away.

Which really means that instead of leaving my desk with a smile and a positive attitude, I leave it with a scowl and my negative energy ruins whatever task I have to attend to.

What an incredible waste of our time and emotions. We know in our heart that jealousy and resentment hurts us, holds us back, and are not pleasing to God. So why do we hold onto them?

This past summer I was training for a 10K run to celebrate my birthday. I was also about 50 lbs overweight. As I ran, I said to myself, 'Imagine how much easier this would be if I wasn't carrying this extra weight.'

In today's verse from Proverbs, God is telling me the same thing. Imagine how much lighter my outlook and attitude would be if I weren't carrying around so much resentment.

When we feel resentment about our present circumstances, we stop ourselves from moving forward. We start feeling resentment towards others…and you know where that leads. Jealousy and resentment are roommates.

When we allow resentment to grow in our hearts, we can feel jealousy towards others who we believe 'have it easier' than we do. Instead of focusing on and working toward our dream, we become obsessed with someone else's progress.

Imagine how much easier it would be to get through our daily tasks and work on the projects that really matter to us if we weren't carrying around that extra load!

How do we lay down the burden of jealousy and resentment?

First, **give it to God in prayer. Tell Him honestly what you are feeling, even if it's ugly. Then, ask for forgiveness.**

Ask for His help with whatever it is that is the focus of your jealousy or resentment. Ask God to help you accept that we are each on our own path.

When I compare my progress toward my dream to someone else, I am diminishing God's plan for my life. I am not fully trusting that God is working everything out for my best life, as long as I am obedient to His Will.

Then, make a list of 5 things that you are grateful for, and focus on them.

Replace your attitude of resentment with an attitude of gratitude.

Rinse (ask for forgiveness) and repeat (create your daily list of gratitude until it becomes second nature).

Where does resentment show up in your life?

Day 23

Therefore, since we are surrounded by such a huge crowd of witnesses to the life of faith,

let us strip off every weight that slows us down,

especially the sin that so easily trips us up.

And **let us run with endurance the race God has set before us.**

~ *Hebrews 12:1*

How joyful are those who fear the Lord

and delight in obeying His commands.

Their children will be successful

everywhere; an entire generation of godly

people will be blessed.

They themselves will be wealthy,

and their good deeds will last

forever.

Those who are righteous will be

long remembered.

They do not fear bad news;

they confidently trust the Lord

to care for them.

They are confident and fearless

and can face their foes triumphantly.

They share freely and give

generously to those in need.

Their good deeds will be

remembered forever.

They will have influence and

honor.

~Psalm 112:1-3, 6-9

Day 23

BELIEVING GOD'S WORD

This morning as I was reading my morning devotions, I thought, 'If I really *believed* that I could count on these promises from God, life would be so much easier.'

Imagine if you could face each day like this:

They do not fear bad news;
they confidently trust the Lord
to care for them.

Or, if you were confident enough to feel like this:

They are confident and fearless
and can face their foes triumphantly.

They share freely and give generously to those in
need.
Their good deeds will be
remembered forever.
They will have influence and honor.

It's difficult to trust God for His provision when we've failed ourselves so many times. 'My dream will never come true,' we think. Or, 'I'll never be a success.'

We read the Bible, and the words sound nice, but we don't believe they apply to us, because we've encountered so much disappointment.

The sad truth is that it's impossible to trust God when we don't fully trust the promises He's made in His Word!

If, like me, you are having a difficult time completely surrendering your trust to God, join me in confessing this lack of trust to God and asking Him to strengthen our hearts.

Dear God,

Please forgive my lack of trust in You and the promises You've clearly provided for us in Your Word.

Lord, I believe in You. Yet my insecurities often keep me from completely surrendering and believing that You will help me, even though Your Word promises You will.

God, I am ashamed to admit this weakness to You. I ask for Your forgiveness, and I pray that You will work in my heart today to strengthen my faith.

I love You, God.

Amen.

Day 24

For God has said,

**"I will never fail you.
I will never abandon you."**

So we can say with confidence,
**"The Lord is my helper,
so I will have no fear.**
What can mere people do to me?"
~ Hebrew 13:5-6

Not to us, O Lord, not to us,
but **to Your name goes all the
glory
for Your unfailing love and
faithfulness.** ~ *Psalm 115:1*

Day 24

GOD NEVER FAILS

On the ride home last night, my car's warning lights started flashing, telling me that I needed to get the car to the repair shop. It sounds like an electrical problem. It sounds very expensive. And there's no room in my carefully constructed budget for 'very expensive' problems right now.

As I sat down to do my devotions this morning, my heart and head were filled with these fearful thoughts and anxiety. **How was I going to deal with another problem on my already full plate?**

Today's verses are what I found waiting for me.

Then I received a gentle reminder that earlier this week God found a way to provide, unexpectedly turning a mistake into the perfectly timed solution.

So often, this is the way God works in our lives. He has a knack for turning a bad situation to our good or sending help at just the right moment, not a moment sooner. I may never know when an answer to prayer is going to arrive, but I know that God will never fail me.

This morning I prayed that I would grow in my trust of His ways enough to not be fearful every time something worrying happens but instead face it with faith and courage.

Dear God,

Please remove fear from our hearts and replace it with Your assurance that You are in control, and that You never fail us.

I love You.

Amen

Day 25

28-30 All this happened to King Nebuchadnezzar. Just twelve months later, he was walking on the balcony of the royal palace in Babylon and boasted, "Look at this, Babylon the great! And **I built it all by myself, a royal palace adequate to display my honor and glory!**"

31-32 The words were no sooner out of his mouth than a voice out of heaven spoke, "This is the verdict on you, King Nebuchadnezzar: Your kingdom is taken from you. You will be driven out of human company and live with the wild animals. You will eat grass like an ox. The sentence is for seven seasons, enough time to learn that the High God rules human kingdoms and puts whomever he wishes in charge."

33 It happened at once. Nebuchadnezzar was driven out of human company, ate grass like an ox, and was soaked in heaven's dew. His hair grew like the feathers of an eagle and his nails like the claws of a hawk.

34-35 "At the end of the seven years, I, Nebuchadnezzar, looked to heaven. I was given my mind back and I blessed the High God, thanking and glorifying God, who lives forever:

"His sovereign rule lasts and lasts, his kingdom never declines and falls. Life on this earth doesn't add up to much, but God's heavenly army keeps everything going. No one can interrupt his work, no one can call his rule into question. **36-37** "At the same time that I was given back my mind, I was also given back my majesty and splendor, making my kingdom shine. All the leaders and important people came looking for me. I was reestablished as king in my kingdom and became greater than ever. **And that's why I'm singing—I, Nebuchadnezzar—singing and praising the King of Heaven:**

"Everything he does is right, and he does it the right way. He knows how to turn a proud person into a humble man or woman." ~ *Daniel 4:28-37 The Message*

Day 25

HONOR GOD

In today's reading, Daniel interprets the dream of a great king who attributed all of his achievements to his own efforts. Daniel warns that unless the king acknowledges God's role in his success, everything he has will be taken from him.

Predictably, the king continues on his own way, until one day when the dream is fulfilled and he is left wandering in the wilderness.

When he eventually comes to the realization of God's role in his life, he falls on his knees and worships God. He gave God the glory, humbled himself, and his kingdom was restored.

So often we attribute our successes in life to our own efforts (and our failures, too). Doesn't it feel good to say, "I did it myself!" We like to see our hard work recognized, because it helps us to feel good about ourselves.

Today's reading was a humbling wake-up call for me.

God certainly appreciates our hard work, and it is essential to achievement. But, like King Nebuchadnezzar, we must acknowledge where our strength and success truly comes from: God, the Source of All.

We need to appreciate God's role in our lives first, give Him the glory, and hand Him our dreams, and all other aspects of our lives, and then go forward from there.

Day 26

I know all the things you do. I have seen
your love, your faith, your service,
and your patient endurance.
And I can see your constant improvement in all these things.
~ *Revelation 2:19*

I am counting on the Lord;
yes, I am counting on Him.
I have put my hope in His word.
~*Psalm 130:5*

$\mathcal{D}$ay 26

GOD SEES YOU

Today's verses are a call and response.

In the first verse we have God's assurance that He hears our prayers, knows our heart's desires, and sees our attempts to live better lives.

I especially like the last line: "And I can see your constant improvement in all these things." Doesn't that sound like the conversational tone you'd love to have with God?

Yes! God is on our side! He's not the judgmental old man with a white beard sitting on a remote throne.

He's our Father, our Counselor, and our Abba. As we can see from this verse, instead of condemning our mistakes, God wants to encourage our growth.

The second verse is our response.

We believe in God's faithfulness, and we respond with our faithfulness to Him.

We can trust Him with our hopes and dreams because of the promises He has spoken to us, through His Word.

These verses reflect the relationship that God calls us toward. He wants us to know that He sees us. He is an active observer of each of our lives. He appreciates our efforts and understands our needs.

God longs for us to bring Him into our lives more actively.

$\mathcal{D}$ay 27

I know all the things you do, and

I have opened a door for you that no

one can close.

You have little strength,

yet you obeyed My word and did not

deny Me.

~ *Revelation 3:8*

$\mathcal{D}$ay 27

GOD'S OPEN DOOR

Today's verse is God's Word of encouragement for our heart's desire, our goals, and our special projects that we are working on.

Many of these projects may take months or even years to come to fruition, but we can remain confident that **when God has opened a door for us, nothing will be able to close it.**

Often we hear that when God closes one door, He opens another. But we get stuck staring at the closed door, certain that it was the one we were destined to walk through. Which is what keeps us from seeing God's open door. We blind ourselves to God's greater vision for our lives.

The key to success is aligning our plans with God's plan for our lives.

The best way to do that is by strengthening our relationship with God, through reading the Bible, and by presenting our plans to God through prayer and watching and listening for His direction as we take action. This is what I mean by waiting *with* God when we are waiting for an answer to prayer.

When we follow God's guidance for our lives, we can rest assured that He will be right there by our side, no matter how long the journey takes us.

Trusting God with our dream becomes an opportunity to grow with God, so that when the answer to our prayer arrives, we find that we are in a better place due to our spiritual maturation.

This verse shows that, even when we have little strength, we can call on God's strength, and He promises to be with us through every hardship and setback.

When we meet with discouragement or setback, we can still find encouragement to keep going, because God has opened a door for us that nothing will be able to close.

$\mathcal{D}$ay 28

"This message is from **the Lord, who stretched out the heavens**, laid the foundations of the earth, and **formed the human spirit**."
~ *Zechariah 12:1*

"Praise the Lord!
Salvation and glory and power
belong to our God."
~ *Revelation 19:1*

How good to sing praises to our God!
How delightful and how fitting!
He heals the brokenhearted
and **bandages their wounds.**
He counts the stars
and calls them all by name.

How great is our Lord!

His Power is absolute!

His understanding is

beyond comprehension!

The Lord supports the humble,

but He brings the wicked down into

the dust.

He covers the heavens with clouds,

provides rain for the earth,

and makes the grass grow in

mountain pastures.

~Psalm 147:1, 3-6,

$\mathcal{D}$ay 28

PRAISE GOD

Sometimes, when I am reading the Bible I am struck simply by the beauty of the images used to portray the magnificence of our mighty God.

I know. I know. I should write about the wonderful assurance these verses provide.

How the same God who counts and names each star in the heavens, knows each of us by name and wants to heal our broken hearts.

And all of that is true.

Our God *makes grass grow in mountain pastures* and wants to provide for our every need.

My heart is filled with gratitude for each and every one of these promises.

My heart is also filled with joy at the beauty of their expression.

One of my great joys in reading the Bible is discovering the beautiful language God has inspired to share His wisdom and love with us. What a gift we have received through the Bible.

We thank You, O God!

We give thanks because You are near.

People everywhere tell of Your wonderful deeds.

~ Psalm 75:1

This might be the greatest reason to read our Bible every day. When we spend regular time with God we draw closer to Him. We can hear Him direct our steps, we can talk to Him about our dreams and hear His input.

When we read the Bible, even for five minutes a day, we can grow in wisdom by hearing God speak to us through His Holy Word.

Will you make a commitment to spend the next seven days reading the Bible each day, for just five minutes?

I believe God will meet you in those pages.

Amen.

What passages in the Bible inspire you with their beauty?

Day 29

Then Jesus said, "**Come to Me, all of you who are weary and carry heavy burdens, and I will give you rest.**

Take My yoke upon you. Let Me teach you, because I am humble
and gentle at heart, and you will find rest for your souls.

For My yoke is easy to bear, and the burden I give you is light.
~ *Matthew 12:28-30*

Day 29

FORWARD WITH GOD

I decided that my word for the New Year would be *Forward*. So I created a list in my journal about what specific steps I needed to move forward in my life so that at the end of the year, I wasn't covering the same territory as last December.

This morning, I read these verses and then read this passage in *Jesus Calling*, by Sarah Young:

Rehearsing your troubles results in experiencing them many times, whereas you are meant to go through them only when they actually occur.

Don't multiply your suffering in this way! Instead, come to Me, and relax in My Peace. I will strengthen you and prepare you for this day, transforming your fear into confident trust.

How often do we rehash the past and worry about the present and future, spending more time worrying than taking action that would resolve the problem?

It seems to me, that Jesus was saying that we need to lay our worries at His Feet and leave them in His capable hands.

The key is, once we leave our prayers with Jesus, we can't go back and pick them up again! We need to leave them behind and be willing to trust that our prayers are heard and will be answered.

When we do this, we will be able to move forward, free and light, with a new perspective on the future.

We are not doomed to repeat the past. We can begin anew each day and choose a new path, taking positive action, and trusting in God for the outcome. Release worry and let God have His perfect way.

Day 30

A Gentile woman who lived there came to Him pleading, "**Have mercy on me, Oh Lord, Son of David!**"

But Jesus gave her no reply, not even a word. Then His disciples urged Him to send her away. "**Tell her to go away," they said. "She is bothering us with all her begging.**"

Then Jesus said to the woman, "I was sent only to help God's lost sheep, the people of Israel."

But she came and worshiped him, pleading again, "Lord, help me!"

Jesus responded, "It isn't right to take food from the children and throw it to the dogs."

She replied, "That's true, Lord, but even dogs are allowed to eat the scraps that fall beneath their master's table."

"Dear woman," Jesus said to her, "your faith is great. Your request is granted." And her daughter was instantly healed.

~ *Matthew 15:22–28*

$\mathcal{D}$ay 30

HOW GREAT
IS YOUR FAITH?

When I first read this parable from today's reading, my initial reaction was 'Wow, Jesus can be exclusionary!' (Okay, actually I thought, 'Wow, why is He being a snob!')

But I don't think that was the point He was making. After all, you'll notice that even when His own disciples tell Him to send the woman away, He doesn't.

After reading the parable again tonight and reflecting on it, I believe that Jesus was teaching us a lesson on the value of persistence in our faith.

When times are tough or we have been working and waiting for a very long time for a breakthrough on something we've committed to prayer but haven't seen a result for, it's easy to give up.

It's easy to say, "Well, God didn't answer my prayer." Or "This wasn't meant to be, so I'm going to stop trying. Stop asking."

Believe me, I've been there. In fact, in some areas of my life, I'm there right now.

Which is why I believe that Jesus is encouraging us to hang in there. Keep praying. Keeping asking. Persistently. Keep working on that dream.

And believe, that in God's perfect time, we too will hear: "Your faith is great. Your request is granted."

Day 31

20 In the morning as Jesus and his disciples walked along, they saw the fig tree. It was dried up all the way down to the roots.

21 Peter remembered. He said to Jesus, "Rabbi, look! The fig tree you put a curse on has dried up!"

22 "Have faith in God," Jesus said.

23 "What I'm about to tell you is true. Suppose one of you says to this mountain, 'Go and throw yourself into the sea.' **You must not doubt in your heart. You must believe that what you say will happen. Then it will be done for you.**

24 "So I tell you, when you pray for something, believe that you have already received it. Then it will be yours.

25/26 And when you stand praying, forgive anyone you have anything against. Then your Father in heaven will forgive your sins."

~ *Mark 11:20-26*

Day 31

SPEAK YOUR FAITH

Do you have faith in your faith?

Do you have the courage to speak your faith aloud?

Again and again, Jesus teaches about how important it is for us to have faith.

Faith in Him.

Faith in God.

And faith in our dream.

In fact, Jesus wants us to have so much faith that we will be willing to speak our dream aloud and then believe that they have been heard by God and will be acted upon.

This is where it gets tricky.

It's easy to pray and ask and hope.

It's a whole lot harder to pray, ask, and believe. To believe so strongly that you are willing to speak your dream out loud.

To believe that God loves your dream as much as you do, and stands ready, right now, today, to work with you on that dream if you will just ask Him.

To have faith that God will provide everything you need to achieve your dream.

That is the unbreakable, mountain-moving faith that I work toward every day. How about you?

That is exactly the faith that Jesus calls us to develop as we walk with Him.

It is a faith that is new every day.

When one prayer is answered, when one dream comes true, another one will take its place.

Which is why our relationship with God grows deeper each day. God meant for our walk with Him to be an adventure that never ends.

God loves you beyond measure and calls you to a deeper relationship with Him.

Speak with God every day. Read His Word. Walk closer with God and watch the amazing things He will do in your life. Can you trust God with your dream?

Yes!

Will you?

That is a question only you can answer. I hope the answer is, yes, yes, yes.!

Let's pray together right now...

Dear God,

Thank you for this time we've shared together. Lord, you know the dreams we carry in our hearts, because you are the author of our story.

We are asking you right now to join us in building these dreams to Your glory. Give us the courage we need to never give up, when challenges come and threaten our dream.

Instead, remind us that we can turn to You for strength and encouragement.

Help us to create lives that reflect Your best for each of us, so that we can fulfill our dreams. We know that when we seek your Will, our heart's desire, is Your heart's desire for us.

We love You, we praise Your Holy Name, and we thank You for each and every day.

In Jesus Name, Amen.

Thank you again for sharing this time together.

God bless you,

Amen.

From The Author

If you enjoyed *Trusting God with Your Dream*, please take a moment to leave a review on **Amazon.com**, **Goodreads.com**, or one of your favorite indie book sites. Sharing your enjoyment of a book helps to spread the word and is more important to an indie-author than anything else!

Keep reading for bonus first chapters from my novels *God Loves You. - Chester Blue*, and *Mrs. Tuesday's Departure*.

God Loves You.

—Chester Blue

By Suzanne Elizabeth Anderson

CHAPTER ONE

"My Goodness, there are so many stars out tonight," Miss Millie whispered. She stood on her back porch, hands on her hips, head tilted back, and stared at the glittering night sky.

Finally, she found her favorite constellation, the Big Dipper. "How lucky we are to have such wondrous stars to enjoy."

Each night she came outside to admire the moon and the blanket of twinkling stars that covered the sky from one end to the other. She'd been doing this for most of her seventy-five years on Earth.

Some nights, the stars formed the shapes of animals romping through the sky, like the Big Dipper, which formed part of the Ursa Major, called that because 'ursa' meant 'bear' and it looked like a big bear in the sky. Which is exactly why it was her favorite. Miss Millie had a very special place in her heart for bears.

For Miss Millie, each night held a new adventure as she watched the stars move across the sky with the changing seasons. And each night she made a wish on the first star she saw. Most nights, Miss Millie's heart was filled with joy at the beauty of the night sky. But tonight was so very different. It was the end of a long day that had brought terrible news. Instead of smiling as she looked at the panorama overhead, she pursed her lips to keep from crying and her eyes filled with tears and blurred the stars she loved so dearly.

Tonight she had a special wish. She walked down the steps of the porch and out to the backyard. The grass was wet and cool beneath her bare feet. Miss Millie looked up at the sky and thought about the right way to phrase her wish. She needed to think carefully, because this wasn't an ordinary wish. It was going to be a prayer. And prayers were more powerful than wishes.

Lately she'd been bothered that the world had forgotten the magic of wishes and dreams. Nowadays, it seemed that people looked down instead of up. They went to work, they came home, and then they went to sleep. It seemed that most people moved through their lives as if they were sleepwalking.

Miss Millie understood how this could easily happen. Some people gave up on their wishes and dreams because they'd been disappointed too many times in life and just didn't have the courage to keep hoping things would change.

That's what had happened in the little Midwestern town where Miss Millie had lived her whole life. It had been a gradual thing, but like rust, some gradual things can be deadly. When she was a little girl, her hometown of Blossom, Ohio, was a vibrant place, full of young families. No matter how many books about faraway places young Millie read, she couldn't imagine living anywhere else.

Which is why, when Miss Millie grew up, she opened a shop on Main Street. Main Street was always filled with beautiful shops and shoppers so it was the perfect place to open a store.

In her shop, Miss Millie sold and repaired all sorts of teddy bears. With all those young families, Miss Millie's shop was always busy. Young children came with their parents to choose their first bear.

Adults came to have their cherished childhood bears fixed after they'd been loved through many years and needed a stitch to repair a tear, or new eyes or ears.

Her shop even attracted teddy bear collectors, who knew that Miss Millie had a secret supply of very old, very special bears that she could sometimes be convinced to sell to a special home.

As the years, and then decades flew by, Miss Millie became known as the best teddy bear historian and repairwoman in the Midwest. Some people said she was even the best in the entire United States.

But then the children of the young families became adults and went off to college. And never returned home to Blossom to start their own families.

At first no one noticed that the shops on Main Street were quieter than usual, or that the Main Street Diner never filled up after the morning rush of farmers who stopped by for breakfast at five a.m.

Even Miss Millie didn't notice at first. She still received a lot of business through the mail, for bears that needed to be repaired, or requests for a search for a rare bear that a collector was hoping to find. But then one day Miss Mille looked up from her table at the back of the shop where she usually spent her day working, and noticed that she was alone.

The next day it was the same. And the day after that. So she went to see her friend, Lulu, the waitress at the Main Street Diner and asked her if she'd also noticed fewer people on Main Street.

"Fewer people, on Main Street?" Lulu threw back her head and laughed.

She laughed so hard, she had to put down the pot of coffee she'd holding to pour Miss Millie's second cup. "Honey, it's not just Main Street, this whole town is as quiet as a church on Monday. So many people have moved away, I believe we're the town that's been forgotten."

Miss Millie looked down at her cup of coffee and frowned. This was terrible news. Blossom was a wonderful town. Yes, it was a small town and perhaps not as exciting as a big city. But there were so many good things about it. Why had people given up and moved away?

That was a month ago. Since that conversation with Lulu, things had gotten worse. Once Miss Millie had started to pay attention, she realized that at times a whole week would go by without a single person coming into her shop. And on her walk home at the end of the day, she began to notice that more and more of the stores that shared Main Street were closing or were already empty.

And then today, Miss Millie had received the worst news of all. Mr. Jones, the man who owned the building, which housed her teddy bear shop, had lost the building to the bank. The bank was going to sell the building at auction, which meant that Miss Millie could no longer have a teddy bear shop in his building. She would have to move.

This was of course terrible news. Not only would Miss Millie lose her shop, she would lose her business. Yes, yes, perhaps she could open a new shop in one of the many other empty stores on Main Street. But this was the proof that it wouldn't matter where she moved, there were simply not enough people in Blossom to shop in her teddy bear store.

Which is why tonight she stood staring up at the stars with a special purpose in her heart. Miss Millie believed in dreams and wishes. And tonight she was going to pray for some way to share her belief with others.

"Dear God," Miss Millie began as she looked up at the stars, "how many people never see how beautiful the sky is at night because they simply don't take the time to look up?"

She smiled as a shooting star flew through the dark sky. "Maybe it's because we seem to be going through a tough time right now. I suppose when times are tough people don't have time for teddy bears or small towns like Blossom. I know that You are the Creator of all things. And I know, when things look the worst is when something new and wonderful is about to happen, if we can just hold on. Now that my teddy bear shop is closed I don't know what I'm going to do. I don't know what's going to happen to my hometown, but You do." Miss Millie said. "Dear God, I'm holding on, but I could sure use a bit of help from You. Give me a way to share the gift of believing in dreams with others, too."

Miss Millie stretched out her arms and embraced all the beauty she saw in the sky above her head. She silently thanked God for creating such a beautiful universe where anything was possible even when it seemed impossible.

She smiled as she saw another star shooting across the sky. "Thank you, God." And she turned and went back in the house to go to bed.

The next morning, Miss Millie woke up early. She climbed from her bed and stretched her arms over her head and then twisted from side to side to get her creaky old bones and muscles warmed up to start the day.

As she turned, she glanced out of her bedroom window, and saw that it was a glorious, sunny, summer morning.

She threw on her robe and hurried downstairs; she needed to make her breakfast and get to the shop. On such a beautiful morning there were certain to be lots of people on Main Street and that meant there might be some new customers for her shop!

Then she stopped on the bottom step and touched her fingertips to her lips as she remembered that her shop was closing. There wouldn't be lots of people on Main Street. So many of the stores were empty, no one came to Main Street anymore. If they needed anything, they went to the big mall, in the big town, down the hill.

Suddenly she felt very sad about closing her store and facing the future alone. What would she do? Miss Millie blinked back the tears. *No,* she thought, *I won't cry, I know that when things are at their worst, something better is just around the corner if we just put one foot in front of the other and keep moving forward.*

She grasped the banister railing tightly and straightened her back with her new resolve. Her heart still hurt, and she was more than a little bit afraid of not knowing what to do next, but she would take her own advice.

Well then, this morning would be the perfect time to work in her garden! She needed to weed the flowerbed and then she would tie up the beans in the vegetable garden. If she was lucky, the cabbage and zucchini would be ready to harvest and she would be able to make soup for tonight's dinner.

Later, she would go to her shop on Main Street and begin packing her teddy bears. She would make a list of all the people she knew who might want to buy one of the remaining bears, then she'd pick a few that she could donate to the children's hospital, and finally, she would bring the rest home. They would sit on the shelves of her office until she figured out what to do next.

First though, she would pick up the newspaper from the front porch, make coffee, have a bite to eat, put on her overalls and her green rubber clogs, and then she'd be ready to work in the garden. She'd finished making her mental list of things to do, just as she opened the front door to pick up her morning newspaper.

Right next to her newspaper, she found a box wrapped in plain brown paper and tied with twine. Miss Millie's name and address was printed in big red letters in the lower right corner. As she looked closer, she noticed there was no return address to be found anywhere. Who had sent the box?

Miss Millie picked up the box and her newspaper and brought them both into the kitchen where she placed them on the table while she made a pot of coffee and a piece of toast for her breakfast.

She carefully cut the piece of toast in half. On one half she spread a spoonful of peanut butter and on the other half she spread a spoonful of chocolate hazelnut spread. This was her favorite breakfast for sunny days. She sat down at the table with her cup of coffee and her plate of toast and carefully considered the box as she ate her breakfast.

She hadn't ordered anything, so that couldn't be it.

She chewed her toast and thought very carefully.

It wasn't her birthday.

She took a sip of coffee, and thought more deeply.

It was the end of August. Schools had just started, perhaps it was a box of notebooks and pencils that were meant for a young student who lived nearby?

Miss Millie checked the address again. No, it was her name and address clearly printed on the front of the box.

Christmas was still four months away.

Perhaps, it was time to stop staring at the box and take action.

Miss Millie moved her cup and plate to the side of the table and placed the box in front of her. Very carefully, she cut the twine and unwrapped the brown paper that covered the box. Beneath the plain brown paper was a cardboard box with a lid. It was a plain orange box with no writing anywhere that might give a hint as to what was inside. So Miss Millie lifted the lid of the box.

And was very surprised by what she saw.

Mrs. Tuesday's Departure

By Suzanne Elizabeth Anderson

Chapter One

"I CAN'T SLEEP Nana."

Mila's skin was clear and pale; like the antique German porcelain dolls I'd bought for her when she was a child. Long dark lashes shaded her almond shaped blue eyes.

I released the doorknob that I'd been ready to close, entered her room and settled into an overstuffed chair with a sigh and a smile that belied my worry. Candlelight silhouetted Mila's face in a halo of pale yellow.

The book she held created a shadow that fell across her chest making the pink roses on her nightgown glow and float in the shadows of her long dark hair.

In the five years that Mila had lived here, there were few nights when I did not find her with a book.

When Mila first arrived, I placed this chair next to her bed to read aloud one of the children's books that provided me with my living and my reputation. Over the years, the chair remained, I wrote more books, and read each one to Mila until she outgrew them and began to read the novels she found in my study. The ritual of our time together before bed, our discussion of books, remained. Even during these years of war.

She propped the book against her chest and watched me expectantly. "You're coming with us aren't you?"

"Of course." I turned from her gaze and smoothed the edge of the comforter wishing our conversation could skim the surface as lightly as my fingers.

"And Aunt Anna?" Mila's eyes searched my face for signs of deception.

"Yes, she seems to understand."

"But she forgets things so quickly," Mila added anxiously. "You know what she's like when she becomes confused."

"We'll sort it out in the morning," I folded my hands in my lap and leaned back in the chair. "She'll come with me."

"Mom's worried she'll slow us down."

"She said that to you?" my voice tightened as I finally looked into her eyes.

Mila looked away. "I overheard Mom and Bela in the kitchen before supper."

"I'll make sure that Anna reaches the station on time."

WITH THAT WE sat among the shadows of the bedroom, neither of us willing to enter the overrun province. My younger sister and her husband resented my care taking of my twin sister.

A year ago, Anna had moved in with us. A nervous breakdown made it impossible for her to continue living alone in her apartment near the university where she had been a poet in residence.

Mila began again. "When I try to talk to Momma she snaps at me."

"She's just concerned about the arrangements for our trip," I offered.

"Sometimes she looks over at Bela before answering me."

"Bela's a difficult man."

"I think she's afraid he might leave without her. Would he do that, Nana?"

"No. He wouldn't leave without her."

I rubbed my hands down the length of my wool skirt to warm them. This room resisted warmth despite the clanking radiators that sat like plump cats hissing and spitting against two of the bedroom walls.

I disdained my younger sister's choice in men. Ilona effortlessly used hypochondria as a defence against any form of housework or childrearing labors. She'd picked her husbands accordingly. Men willing to care for her in exchange for total control of her movements and her affections. Jealous masters.

As a result of Ilona's disposition, and the low wages Bela received as a legal clerk, they'd come to live with me after my husband died. They insisted they were concerned about my living alone. Though I surmised my spacious apartment was a greater priority to them than my welfare.

My husband and I lived in a large three-bedroom apartment in the center of Pest. I kept the master bedroom that I'd shared with my husband, which still held his clothes, and his scent.

There were two smaller bedrooms. Mila slept in one, my sister Anna in the other. Ilona and Bela felt those bedrooms were too small for them, and when they realized that I was not going to relinquish the room I'd shared with my husband, they claimed the living room as the only room large enough to accommodate them comfortably.

As a result, my study became both a library and a living room. The dining room and kitchen remained, as they were when my husband and I lived alone here. I maintained the truce with Ilona and endured the angry outbursts of her husband to keep Mila near. She was the daughter I'd always wanted. She was an inquisitive and beautiful young girl.

"What are you reading?" I leaned forward and gestured toward her book, hoping an old routine would bring comfort and distract us from our separate worries.

"Aunt Anna's poems," Mila said, turning the cover toward me. "I can't believe that she wrote the words."

"Before her illness, Anna was a brilliant poet with an enormous gift for making the mundane sublime. She was a remarkable woman. She still is."

"I wish I could talk to her about the poems," Mila said.

"Try," I said. "There are moments when she still understands a great deal."

Mila pushed herself up in the bed and leaned toward me. "What does she remember?"

"For her, the poems that were written a decade ago are the freshest in her mind. That's some of her best work. She can still tell you exactly what she was trying to achieve in each line. Ironically, it's her inability to process what she did yesterday, or a moment ago, that keeps her from creating. It's sad. I know she has so much more to say."

Mila leaned back against the pillows and chewed her lip. "Does she realize what's happening to her?"

I took Mila's hand in mine and gently squeezed it. "She knows."

A year ago, Anna had handed me a stack of leather-bound books. The journals contained Anna's notes on poems that she had struggled through, political skirmishes at the university, and embarrassingly detailed notes on her love life. Anna asked me to edit them and publish them for her.

It was one of the first things she asked for when the doctor concluded that her delusional bouts would become more frequent over time. She wanted some testimony to survive as her real self slipped away. I'd begun working on them when my own writing stalled. I was piqued, discomfited, and touched by what I read. In the long sloping lines of confession that covered the pages of her journals, I realized a depth to her I'd never imagined.

"How long will she recognize us, Nana?"

"I hope forever."

Some things a young girl should not have to learn too quickly. The irony of life, that insanity should take the one thing that allowed Anna to express her greatest gift. I shook my head.

No, that was the least of it. There was so much more I was trying to protect Mila from. Outside her windows, four floors above the street, the March wind moaned.

The windows rattled and whistled softly as cold air seeped through cracks in the warped wooden frames. The streets were unusually quiet. Even at this hour, Budapest should have been alive with the sounds of the city. But there were no cars on the street or pedestrians making their way home from the opera house or the cafe. What a sharp contrast to the celebrations held just days before.

For the rest of Chester Blue's adventures:

God Loves You. - Chester Blue

If you're interested in historical fiction:

Mrs. Tuesday's Departure

For contests, giveaways, and updates on future books, please stop by my home on the Internet:

www.suzanneelizabethanderson.com

God bless you,

Suzanne

Made in the USA
Charleston, SC
10 November 2015